Make:

Geek Girl's Guide to Geek Women

DIY Projects from Four Women Who Pushed the Boundaries of Technology

LYNN BEIGHLEY

Maker Media, Inc
San Francisco

Published by Maker Media, Inc.,
1700 Montgomery Street, Suite 240,
San Francisco, CA 94111

Maker Media books may be purchased for educational, business, or
sales promotional use. Online editions are also available for most titles
(safaribooksonline.com). For more information, contact our corporate/
institutional sales department: 800-998-9938 or *corporate@oreilly.com*.

Publisher: Roger Stewart
Editor: Patrick DiJusto
Copy Editor: Elizabeth Welch, Happenstance Type-O-Rama
Proofreader: Scout Festa, Happenstance Type-O-Rama
Interior Designer and Compositor: Maureen Forys,
Happenstance Type-O-Rama
Cover Designer: Maureen Forys, Happenstance Type-O-Rama

September 2017: First Edition

Revision History for the First Edition

2017-09-13 First Release

See *oreilly.com/catalog/errata.csp?isbn=9781680454994* for release details.

978-1-680-45499-4

Safari® Books Online

Safari Books Online is an on-demand digital library that delivers expert content in both book and video form from the world's leading authors in technology and business. Technology professionals, software developers, web designers, and business and creative professionals use Safari Books Online as their primary resource for research, problem solving, learning, and certification training. Safari Books Online offers a range of plans and pricing for enterprise, government, education, and individuals. Members have access to thousands of books, training videos, and prepublication manuscripts in one fully searchable database from publishers like O'Reilly Media, Prentice Hall Professional, Addison-Wesley Professional, Microsoft Press, Sams, Que, Peachpit Press, Focal Press, Cisco Press, John Wiley & Sons, Syngress, Morgan Kaufmann, IBM Redbooks, Packt, Adobe Press, FT Press, Apress, Manning, New Riders, McGraw-Hill, Jones & Bartlett, Course Technology, and hundreds more. For more information about Safari Books Online, please visit us online.

How to Contact Us

Please address comments and questions to the publisher:

Maker Media
1700 Montgomery St.
Suite 240
San Francisco, CA 94111

You can send comments and questions to us by email at books@ makermedia.com.

Maker Media unites, inspires, informs, and entertains a growing community of resourceful people who undertake amazing projects in their backyards, basements, and garages. Maker Media celebrates your right to tweak, hack, and bend any Technology to your will. The Maker Media audience continues to be a growing culture and community that believes in bettering ourselves, our environment, our educational system—our entire world. This is much more than an audience, it's a worldwide movement that Maker Media is leading. We call it the Maker Movement.

To learn more about Make: visit us at *makezine.com*. You can learn more about the company at the following websites:

Maker Media: *makermedia.com*

Maker Faire: *makerfaire.com*

Maker Shed: *makershed.com*

Maker Share: *makershare.com*

*For inspiring and
creative women everywhere,
including Ada, Anna,
Hildegard, and Mária*

CONTENTS

PREFACE

FOUR WOMEN WHO MADE THE WORLD BETTER

You're about to meet four amazing women who invented and created things and pushed technology forward. After you meet them, you'll get a taste of what they went through. You'll create a secret language, learn how to think like a programmer, make sun-powered images, and use the sun to remove salt from seawater. After you learn about the lives and inventions of these great women, we hope that you'll keep learning and create your own inventions to make the world better!

ACKNOWLEDGMENTS

Thanks to the great team at Maker Media putting this book together, including Maureen Forys, Liz Welch, and Scout Festa.

Extra special thanks to my editor, Patrick DiJusto, for coming up with the idea for this book, giving me the opportunity to write it, and helping me every step of the way.

ADA LOVELACE,
Inventor of the Algorithm

While other visitors gazed at the working of this beautiful instrument with the sort of expression, and I dare say the sort of feeling, that some savages are said to have shown on first seeing a looking-glass or hearing a gun—if, indeed, they had as strong an idea of its marvellousness—Miss Byron, young as she was, understood its working, and saw the great beauty of the invention.

SOPHIA ELIZABETH DE MORGAN, Ada's math tutor

We use computers constantly in our daily lives, but have you ever wondered who invented the very first computer program?

WHO WAS ADA LOVELACE?

Ada Lovelace is widely considered to be the creator of the first computer program. In the 1840s, she was the first person to describe what we now think of as modern computing. She imagined intelligent machines that could do everything from controlling industrial machinery to making music. These are things we use computers for every day!

FIGURE 1.1: Ada Lovelace, the Enchantress of Numbers (1815–1852)

In her day she was known as Augusta Ada King-Noel, Countess of Lovelace. Even back then, the smartest people in the land recognized her talent and skill. Some people even called her "The Enchantress of Numbers."

THE EARLY YEARS

Ada Lovelace was born Ada Gordon in England on December 10, 1815. She was the only child of Lady Anne Isabella Milbanke Byron and George Noel Gordon, better known by his title, Lord Byron. Her parents couldn't have been more opposite, and their marriage was short and very unhappy.

Her father, Lord Byron, was a famous poet during his lifetime and today. But he also had a terrible reputation because of his many debts and scandalous behavior. He also sympathized with the Luddites.

Who Were the Luddites?

The Luddites were a group of men who felt that technology was taking away their jobs. Groups of these Luddites would gather together and smash the industrial machines used to make textiles in parts of England. These men were trying to destroy machines that replaced them in their jobs.

Since Ada's time, technology and computing have shifted the ways many people work. Most manufacturing is now automated, and more and more jobs are being taken over by computers and robots. On the other hand, jobs for people who create the computer programs and technology have exploded.

Ada's mother, nicknamed Anabella, was very religious. She was also a mathematician who focused on order and logic. Byron called Anabella "the princess of parallelograms," but he didn't mean it as a compliment.

After a 12-month marriage, and when Ada was only a few weeks old, Byron told Anabella to leave their home and take Ada with her. Byron never saw his daughter again. He died when Ada was 8.

Anabella was angry. She didn't want Ada to be like her father. She watched over Ada's education, hiring private tutors to teach her science and mathematics. At the time, it was very unusual for a girl to be taught these subjects. Many people in those days believed that women didn't have brains that could understand math and science!

As Ada grew up, she met and learned from many brilliant minds of her time, including Charles Dickens, Michael Faraday, and, most importantly, Charles Babbage.

ADA AND THE ANALYTICAL ENGINE

The most important person Ada met was Charles Babbage. Babbage was an engineer, philosopher, mathematician, and economist and is considered to be the inventor of the computer.

Ada and Babbage met at a meeting where Babbage talked about his invention, the Difference Engine. This was a machine that could calculate mathematical tables. Ada, who loved mathematics, was fascinated.

Why Does Ada Inspire You?

We asked Limor Fried, owner of adafruit.com, why she is inspired by Ada Lovelace.

Who isn't inspired by Lady Ada? Her scientific mind envisioned the computer program before proper computers existed. My favorite story is how she loved gambling and tried to apply her math training to model horse races (turns out it is not so simple!).

Limor "ladyada" Fried, adafruit.com

ADA INVENTS THE FIRST COMPUTER PROGRAM

Babbage kept working and improving on the Difference Engine. He built a far more complicated machine that he called the *Analytical Engine*.

Babbage talked about his invention in Turin, Italy, which inspired a famous Italian scientist to publish a paper about it in 1842. Since Ada was fluent in Italian and understood the machine, Babbage asked her to translate the paper. She did, and she added her own notes and ideas, resulting in a paper that was three times longer than the original!

Ada wrote the first computer program for the Analytical Engine. This computer program was designed to compute something called Bernoulli numbers, a complex mathematical series that's tedious to calculate.

Ada created a set of instructions that told the Analytical Engine how to figure out the correct series of Bernoulli numbers every time. A set of steps like this is called an *algorithm*.

What Is an Algorithm?

An algorithm is a set of instructions. That's it! For example, directions you have to follow to install a game on your computer or recipes to cook something can be considered algorithms.

But we don't call these things algorithms because we mainly use the word to mean a *set of instructions given to a computer*, written in words the computer understands.

Algorithms for computers are usually written in code. By *code*, we mean a special set of words and symbols that computers can understand.

(continues)

(continued)

Here's an example of a simple algorithm written in English. This algorithm is a set of instructions to add two numbers together and then show the sum:

The first number is 10.

The second number is 20.

Add the first number and second number together.

Write down the sum of the two numbers.

If you wanted to write this algorithm in code, you could use a programming language called JavaScript. The code might look like this:

```
var num1 = 10;
var num2 = 20;
document.write(num1 + num2);
```

You can almost read it in English. It's saying:

Take the first number, 10, and save it with the name num1.

Take the second number, 20, and save it with the name num2.

Write the number you get when you add the numbers you stored in num1 and num2.

Ada once wrote that "the Analytical Engine weaves algebraic patterns just as a textile loom weaves flowers and leaves."

What she meant is that, given the right input information, you could make the Analytical Engine solve whatever you wanted it to, such as the result to an equation, a pattern for a rug, or even music.

As long as you can create the right set of instructions, the right algorithm, using computer code, a computer can produce whatever you want.

HOW TO THINK LIKE A COMPUTER PROGRAMMER

In these exercises, you'll start thinking like a programmer!

Before any computer programmer can create a program, she has to think about what the algorithm needs to do in plain English.

There's not enough room in this book to teach you how to create computer code. But you can learn to think like a computer. *You'll find solutions to these problems in the Appendix.*

What you need:

➤ Paper

➤ Pencil

Traveling Through a Maze

Imagine you are trying to give instructions to a simple robot to get through this maze. You might be surprised by just how many directions it needs.

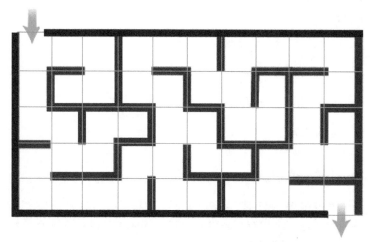

FIGURE 1.2: Write an algorithm to get through the maze.

Part 1

Suppose you want to write an algorithm to travel from the red arrow to the green arrow in Figure 1.2. You can use only these three instructions:

→ go forward 1 square

→ turn right

→ turn left

Part 2

Now imagine that you can use these instructions; how would your algorithm change?

→ go forward *X* squares (*X* can be any number of squares)

→ turn right

→ turn left

Part 3

Now try it with these instructions:

→ go forward X squares

→ turn right and go forward X squares

→ turn left and go forward X squares

Deciding What to Wear

Did you know that algorithms can make decisions based on information? Try to write an algorithm that tells you what to take with you based on the weather.

→ When it rains, you take an umbrella.

➤ When it is sunny, you take your bike.

➤ When it is snowing, you take a coat.

Use only these words and phrases and write an algorithm to decide what to take. You may use some of these more than once.

➤ then take

➤ if

➤ umbrella

➤ rainy

➤ coat

➤ sunny

➤ snowing

➤ or else if

➤ weather =

➤ bike

When you put these together, it will look a lot like computer code. The word "if" is used in many programming languages.

ANNA ATKINS,
First Woman Photographer

The difficulty of making accurate drawings of objects as minute as many of the Algae and Conferae, has induced me to avail myself of Sir John Herschel's beautiful process of Cyanotype, to obtain impressions of the plants themselves, which I have much pleasure in offering to my botanical friends.

ANNA ATKINS, from her book titled *Photographs of British Algae: Cyanotype Impressions*

When you pick up a really old book, a book published in the early 1800s or even earlier, any illustrations in it will be drawings. Consider a book about birds trying to describe how a robin looks different from a bluejay. A talented artist would take days and days to create accurate drawings of each one of the birds. These days, we can just include photos!

One of the first people to recognize that photographic techniques were superior to scientific drawings was Anna Atkins.

WHO WAS ANNA ATKINS?

Anna Atkins was a botanist, a scientist who studies plants. Many historians consider her to have been the first female photographer. She was also the very first person to publish a book illustrated with photographs. Her cyanotypes, an early type of photograph, were used to illustrate her books about plants.

FIGURE 2.1: Anna Atkins (1799–1871), first woman photographer

THE EARLY YEARS

Anna Atkins was born in England in 1799. Anna's mother died when she was born, so her father made sure she learned about science. In Anna's time, it was unusual for a girl to get much education in science. But her father, John Children, was a well-known scientist, and thought it was important for her to learn. He studied mechanics, mineralogy, astronomy, and biology. There's even a butterfly named after him!

Her father had a large scientific laboratory in their home, so it's likely that Anna often visited it and helped him with his experiments. She also got to meet leading English scientists of the day when they visited her father.

Her early work in science was helping her father. She was a talented artist, and one of her first projects was to create amazing scientific drawings to illustrate his English translation of a famous science book, *Genera of Shells*. She began collecting plant specimens and contributing them to museums.

She became famous for her work. Even though it was rare for a woman to be admitted to scientific societies, she became a member of the Botanical Society of London.

ANNA DISCOVERS PHOTOGRAPHY

Both Anna's father and the man she married, John Pelly Atkins, were friends of photographer and inventor William Henry Fox Talbot. Historians think Talbot introduced Anna to the techniques she would come to use in her books.

Anna was one of the first women to take an interest in photography. She realized that using photos of the plants she wanted to write about would be more accurate and faster than drawing them. She bought her first camera in 1841.

Anna decided she would use images in her book *Photographs of British Algae: Cyanotype Impressions*.

FIGURE 2.2: Cyanotype of ferns

Anna created lots of cyanotype illustrations and wrote more books. Sometimes she collaborated with her friend Anne Dixon, a cousin of writer Jane Austen.

GEEK GIRL'S GUIDE TO GEEK WOMEN

What Is a Cyanotype?

A cyanotype is a type of photographic image. The technique was discovered in 1842 by one of Anna's friends, Sir John Herschel. Cyanotypes were first used to make copies of architectural and mechanical drawings. This is where the term *blueprint* comes from!

To create a cyanotype, a surface, usually paper, is coated with two chemical solutions. Then an object to be copied is placed on top, and the paper is exposed to sunlight. After the paper has been exposed to light, it can be quickly rinsed in water to stop the chemical process and capture the image.

Create a Cyanotype

It's fun and easy to create your own cyanotypes of leaves or other small objects with interesting shapes. You'll need a sunny day outside and a shady room inside to get the best results.

What you need:

➜ Sun print paper (you can find this on Amazon by searching for *sun print paper*)

➜ A sunny day

➜ A shady room

➜ Leaves, buttons, rubber bands, or other flat objects with interesting shapes

➜ Water in a sink or cake pan

➜ 2 pieces of cardboard slightly bigger than your sun print paper

→ A few drops of lemon juice (optional)

→ Clear pane of glass or Plexiglas (optional)

Using Pretreated Sun Print Paper

One of the chemicals used to create cyanotypes is highly toxic in its liquid form. Because of this hazard, this experiment uses a safe form of "sun print" paper that you can find for sale online or in craft stores.

Step 1

Prepare the water bath.

Even though the last step is rinsing your paper, you should have the water ready in advance. Add a few inches of water to a stopped-up sink or a large cake pan.

Optional: Adding a few drops of lemon juice to the water will make the final blue color of your cyanotype a little darker.

Step 2

Organize what you're going to put in your print.

You want to expose your sun print paper to light only when you're ready to make your print. Before you take out the sun print paper, spend a few minutes planning how you want to place your objects.

Step 3

Place a piece of cardboard on the table, and have a second piece close by.

FIGURE 2.3: Planning your cyanotype

Step 4

Prepare your sun print.

In a shady room, open the packet of sun print paper and take one sheet out. Put it on the cardboard. Working quickly, place the objects you want to print on the paper. If you have a piece of glass or Plexiglas, place that over the objects to hold them in place on the paper.

Step 5

Cover everything with the second piece of cardboard.

Carefully put the second piece of cardboard on top. This will keep the light off the paper until you're able to put it down outside.

FIGURE 2.4: Objects under Plexiglas

Step 6

Carry the two sheets of cardboard with your sun print paper outside and place them in the sun.

Step 7

Gently remove the top piece of cardboard.
   Very quickly adjust your objects if they've shifted! Hurry!

Step 8

Expose your sun print paper to the sun for a few minutes and watch as the paper changes color to a really light blue.

Step 9

Quickly remove the items and rinse your sun print paper in water for 30 seconds.

FIGURE 2.5: Sun print paper exposed to sunlight

FIGURE 2.6: Rinsing the paper

Step 10

Lay the paper flat to dry.

The print will gradually dry and darken. After it's completely dry, you can put it between the pages of a heavy book for a few days to flatten it out.

FIGURE 2.7: The final print

MORE PROJECTS

Now that you know how to make cyanotypes, here are more projects you can try with the sun print paper you have left:

➤ Experiment with exposing the paper for different lengths of time.

➤ Try creating a cyanotype of something taller than a leaf. You have to be careful to do this only when the sun is high in the sky, or you'll end up capturing big shadows!

➤ You can use a cyanotype to capture the shadow of an object. In the morning or evening, when the sun is lower, place an object on a sidewalk and observe its shadow. If you like the way it looks, get your sun print paper placed with cardboard on top, and when your shadow is in the right spot, move the cardboard.

➤ Try creating two nearly identical cyanotypes, one with lemon juice in the water bath, and one without lemon juice. How are they different after they dry?

➤ Use letters or other shapes that you cut out of cardboard or dark construction paper.

HILDEGARD VON BINGEN,
Secret Language Inventor

When I was forty-two years and seven months old, Heaven was opened and a fiery light of exceeding brilliance came and permeated my whole brain, and inflamed my whole heart and my whole breast, not like a burning but like a warming flame, as the sun warms anything its rays touch.

HILDEGARD VON BINGEN, from her
illustrated work titled *Scivias*

Even though Hildegard had a life full of illness and isolation, she overcame all this to become a famous and well-respected healer, author, composer, and artist during the Middle Ages.

WHO WAS HILDEGARD VON BINGEN?

Hildegard was a creative visionary. She wrote about philosophy, religion, astronomy, and medicine. She gave advice to popes, kings, and other famous leaders of her day. She wrote beautiful music, put her mystic visions in books, wrote plays, and invented her own secret language.

But here's the surprise: Hildegard created amazing things *even though she was trapped in a small room most of her life and not able to go outside!*

FIGURE 3.1: Hildegard von Bingen (1098–1179)

THE EARLY YEARS

Hildegard was the 10th child in a wealthy family. When she was still a toddler, she had what she later called "visions." She said that when she was 3 years old, she "saw so great a brightness that my soul trembled; yet because of my infant condition I could express nothing of it." Some historians think that her visions were caused by the awful migraine headaches she had her whole life.

Her parents were religious and practiced tithing, which meant that they gave 1/10th of everything they owned to the church. This even included their children! Since Hildegard was their 10th child, her parents gave her to the church when she was only 8 years old. That seems hard to imagine, but it gets worse. Hildegard was *enclosed* in a stone room with a very religious girl of 14 named Jutta.

What Does *Enclosed* Mean?

Okay, this part of Hildegard's story is hard to understand with our modern way of thinking. Extremely religious women, or sometimes men, would ask to be permanently sealed up with stone and mortar in a room built into the wall of a church. This room, called an *anchorhold*, had two or three small windows where food could be passed in and through which the person inside could talk to visitors. But she could never leave. These people were called "anchorites." They spent most of their time giving advice to church visitors, sewing, singing, and in prayer. The practice of enclosure was common in Hildegard's time.

Hildegard was closed up in one of these anchorholds when she was just 8 years old! She did have Jutta to keep her company. Jutta taught her basic Latin, how to chant Psalms, and musical skills.

Hildegard also spent her time teaching herself from the books the monks would bring her. Her clever mind and imagination helped her deal with her confinement.

Hildegard remained locked in a cell with Jutta until Jutta died in 1136. Hildegard was 42 years old when she was finally released from the cell. She remained with the church as the leader, or abbess, of a group of nuns the rest of her life, but she spent as much time as she could outside, enjoying nature.

HILDEGARD'S CREATIONS AND INVENTIONS

Hildegard began making a name for herself as a visionary around the time she was allowed out of the anchorhold. She would occasionally speak about otherworldly things that seemed strange to others and even predict future events. When she was walled up, she told these things only to Jutta. But when she was finally free of the cell at age 42, Hildegard began to experience "painful pressures" that led her to believe she needed to reveal her visions to others. One of her friends, a monk, had her write down her visions. The church and the pope decided her visions were genuine. They said Hildegard's visions were "the gift of prophecy which the prophets of old had proclaimed."

Once the pope approved of her words, Hildegard knew everyone else would as well. She started writing to all the most famous leaders of the world, giving them advice. And people listened to her, not just because the pope approved. She knew a lot about everything, from a deep understanding of religion to how to heal various illnesses. She wrote gorgeously illustrated books about God and the universe. She also wrote about medicine and the human body. She published recipes for tinctures and herbal potions for physicians.

And that's not all. Hildegard von Bingen wrote and directed plays. She was the inventor of an entirely new type of drama for the time, the morality play, where the characters represent ideas like hope, virtue, victory, and charity. And she enjoyed toying with words and language so much that she came up with a new way to communicate with her fellow nuns.

HILDEGARD'S SECRET LANGUAGE

Hildegard invented a secret language. She called it Lingua Ignota, "unknown language" in Latin. No one knows why she invented Lingua Ignota. Some people think she might have used it to keep secrets with the other nuns she lived with. She might have thought it was fun to have a secret language with her friends!

Figure 3.2 shows the characters, or glyphs, she made up to stand for the letters of the alphabet.

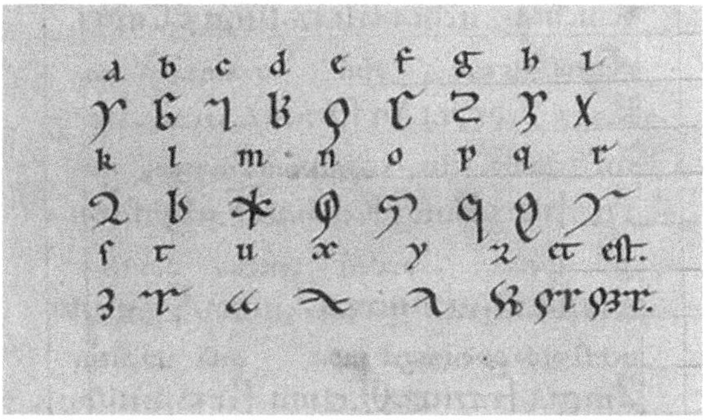

FIGURE 3.2: Hildegard's secret alphabet

Once Hildegard came up with this alphabet, she also invented a lot of new words and created a dictionary of the words she'd made up. For example, *Scorinz* meant "heart," *inimois* meant "human being," and *zunzial* meant "child."

To make it even trickier to figure out, she wrote these words with the letters from her secret alphabet. Linguists today still don't know for sure what some of her words mean!

Why Is Hildegard's Alphabet Missing Letters?

In Hildegard's time, the letters *j*, *v*, and *w* didn't exist.

Invent a Secret Language

Are you ready to create a secret language that only you and your friends can use? You can use emojis to create both secret characters and secret words.

What you need:

➺ Paper

➺ Pencil

➺ A list of emojis that you and your friends use (you'll find a list of common ones here: *https://commons.wikimedia.org/wiki/Emoji*)

Step 1

Make a grid for your alphabet. To begin, draw a grid on a piece of paper with all the letters of the alphabet. Leave a blank square under each letter where you can put your own emoji.

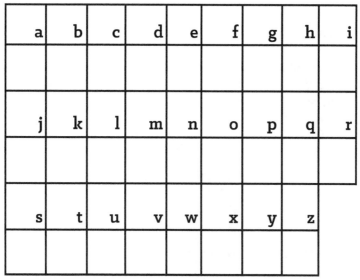

a	b	c	d	e	f	g	h	i
j	k	l	m	n	o	p	q	r
s	t	u	v	w	x	y	z	

FIGURE 3.3: A grid for your secret alphabet

Step 2

The next step is to fill in your alphabet with emojis. For each square in your grid, add an emoji.

Make your alphabet tricky. Try to use emojis that remind you of each letter while not being too obvious. For example, you could use a heart for *h*, but most people would guess that. Instead, you could use a heart for *c* because it reminds you of a candy box. If you use things only you and your friends know, your alphabet will be even harder for strangers to figure out.

Step 3

The next step is to create emoji-based words for your language.

Having an emoji alphabet is great, but it can make for very long sentences when you have to spell out every word. Instead, you can create new words by combining two or three emoji together. The trick to this comes from a Celtic idea known as a *kenning*.

What Is a Kenning?

A kenning consists of two combined words that mean something new. For example, *whale-road* could mean the sea and *sky-candle* could mean the sun. Kennings were first used in the Old Norse language and later in Old English.

So, taking the idea of kenning, you can use two emojis together to represent a new thing. Here are some examples:

→ angry face + pencil = homework

→ cat + sun = taking a nap

→ baby + money = babysitting

The following graphic shows kennings with emojis:

Step 4

In this step, you'll put it all together.

Use your emoji language for spelling out names and places and your emoji kennings for simple nouns. You can also mix in English words to simplify your message while still not giving away your secret.

MÁRIA TELKES,
Sun Queen

Sunlight will be used as a source of energy sooner or later. Why wait?

—MÁRIA TELKES

Imagine you are on a lifeboat in the middle of the ocean, waiting for rescue. You can survive quite a while without food, and you may even manage to figure out how to catch fish to eat. But without fresh water, you won't last very long.

Mária Telkes invented a small, portable device that turns undrinkable seawater into fresh water to help a person survive until rescued.

WHO WAS MÁRIA TELKES?

Mária Telkes was a scientist who had expert knowledge of chemistry, biology, physics, and metallurgy. She was very interested in the transfer of energy in both living and nonliving systems.

FIGURE 4.1: Mária Telkes, inventor and scientist (1900–1995) NYWT&S STAFF PHOTO BY AL RAVENNA

THE EARLY YEARS

Mária Telkes was born in 1900 in Budapest, Hungary. When she was still in high school she became interested in trying to use the power of the sun—solar energy—in new ways. She earned a bachelor's degree and a Ph.D. in physical chemistry in Hungary and began teaching at a university there.

When she was 25, she came to the United States to visit a relative. During her visit, the Cleveland Clinic Foundation offered her a job as a biophysicist. Mária decided to stay in the U.S. and take this job. She began working on projects that sounded like science fiction at the time. She and her boss came up with a method to measure brain waves, the tiny amounts of electricity put out by the human brain. She also studied how cells become cancerous.

Mária's Solar Inventions

In 1939, Mária went to work for MIT on their Solar Energy Conversion Project. While working there, she developed a solar-powered still that could turn seawater into fresh, drinkable water. The still was small enough to store on lifeboats. The design was so effective that larger versions of the solar still have provided fresh drinking water for the entire Virgin Islands. Mária's invention saved the lives of many men in the Navy whose ships went down during World War II.

Mária went on to do more with solar power. In 1948, she created the world's first completely solar-heated house. This house had an outer glass layer with an inside layer made of metal. The sun heated the air between the layers. The metal layer absorbed the heat and electric fans spread the air around, warming the house.

Mária also invented solar ovens for cooking food. These ovens are inexpensive so that people in developing countries can use them. She also developed solar dryers, water heaters, and materials that can handle the temperature extremes of outer space.

Because she was interested in solar power when she was young, she was able to learn everything she needed from many different fields of study to invent new things. She held seven patents for methods of heat storage as well as heating and cooling technologies. The scientific community recognized her important contributions to solar technology, and in 2012, Mária Telkes was inducted into the National Inventors Hall of Fame. Mária never stopped learning and continued to work and teach well into her nineties.

What Is a Solar Still?

One of Mária's most famous inventions is the *solar distillation water purifier* (also called a solar still). She created it to help people stranded in the ocean turn seawater into water they could drink to survive.

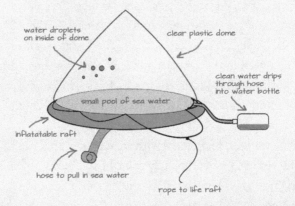

water droplets on inside of dome

clear plastic dome

clean water drips through hose into water bottle

small pool of sea water

inflatatable raft

hose to pull in sea water

rope to life raft

The solar still consists of a clear plastic dome on top of a small inflatable platform. The platform has a hose at the bottom to let in seawater. The sun shines through the plastic dome and causes the water to evaporate and condense to form droplets on the dome, leaving the salt behind. The droplets drip down the sides of the dome into a trench. This trench drains into a hose that fills up a water bottle. A person stranded on a life raft can drink this water and survive.

Create a Solar Still

You can use the sun to turn salty water into clean, safe-to-drink water.

What you need:

- A sunny day
- Large cake pan
- Small bowl or glass that is shorter than the cake pan
- Plastic wrap
- Large rubber band
- 1 cup of water
- Small rock
- 1 tablespoon of salt
- Tea bag (optional)
- Black garbage bag (optional)

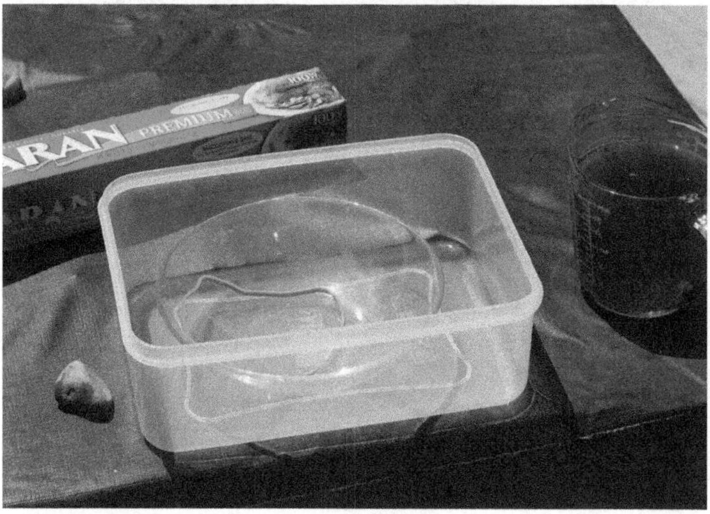

FIGURE 4.2: What you'll need to create a solar still

Step 1

To create your seawater, add salt to a cup of very warm water and stir. If you drop a tea bag in your warm salty water for a few minutes, it will color the water brown. As your water is treated by solar power evaporation, the color of the tea will also be left behind from the resulting clean water.

Step 2

Pour the salt water into the cake pan.

Step 3

Place an empty glass bowl inside the cake pan.

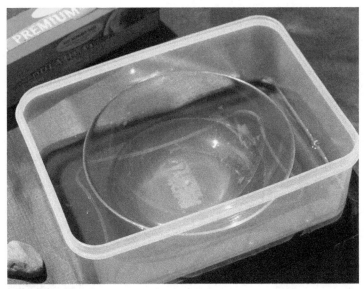

FIGURE 4.3: Glass bowl to catch the clean water

Step 4

Tear off a piece of plastic wrap and put it over the cake pan; secure the wrap with the rubber band.

FIGURE 4.4: Cover the solar still with plastic.

Step 5

Place a weight, such as a rock, on the plastic to create an angle. If you place the rock or other small weight directly above the glass bowl, the water droplets that form will be more likely to drip into the bowl. In our design, the drops will flow inward. In Mária's still, they flow to the outside, where they're trapped in a gutter.

Step 6

Place the still in the direct sunlight and wait.

If you place your solar still on a black surface, such as a black garbage bag, the evaporation process will happen more quickly.

FIGURE 4.5: Add a weight to create an inverted dome.

FIGURE 4.6: Small drops of condensation begin to form.

Step 7

After several hours, check to see how much clean water has collected in the glass cup.

The pan gives the solar energy a large surface area. In Mária's solar still, this is similar to the bottom of the floating raft that holds seawater. Feel free to taste the water. It shouldn't be salty, and, if you used a tea bag, you should notice that the water is clear again.

Appendix
Answers to Chapter 1 Exercises

TRAVELING THROUGH A MAZE SOLUTION

Part 1

To get through the maze, you have to move forward 33 times and make 11 turns to the right and 11 turns to the left. You have to use 55 total commands. Here's the order:

1. go forward 1 square
2. go forward 1 square
3. go forward 1 square
4. turn left
5. go forward 1 square
6. turn right
7. go forward 1 square
8. turn right
9. go forward 1 square
10. turn left
11. go forward 1 square
12. turn left
13. go forward 1 square
14. go forward 1 square

15. go forward 1 square

16. turn left

17. go forward 1 square

18. turn right

19. go forward 1 square

20. turn left

21. go forward 1 square

22. go forward 1 square

23. turn left

24. go forward 1 square

25. turn right

26. go forward 1 square

27. turn right

28. go forward 1 square

29. go forward 1 square

30. turn right

31. go forward 1 square

32. turn left

33. go forward 1 square

34. turn left

35. go forward 1 square

36. turn right

37. go forward 1 square

38. go forward 1 square

39. go forward 1 square

40. turn right

41. go forward 1 square

42. turn right

43. go forward 1 square

44. turn left

45. go forward 1 square

46. go forward 1 square

47. turn right

48. go forward 1 square

49. turn left

50. go forward 1 square

51. turn left

52. go forward 1 square

53. go forward 1 square

54. turn right

55. go forward 1 square

Part 2

This time you need only 45 commands:

1. go forward 3 squares	21. go forward 1 square
2. turn left	22. turn right
3. go forward 1 square	23. go forward 2 squares
4. turn right	24. turn right
5. go forward 1 square	25. go forward 1 square
6. turn right	26. turn left
7. go forward 1 square	27. go forward 1 square
8. turn left	28. turn left
9. go forward 1 square	29. go forward 1 square
10. turn left	30. turn right
11. go forward 3 squares	31. go forward 3 squares
12. turn left	32. turn right
13. go forward 1 square	33. go forward 1 square
14. turn right	34. turn right
15. go forward 1 square	35. go forward 1 square
16. turn left	36. turn left
17. go forward 2 squares	37. go forward 2 squares
18. turn left	38. turn right
19. go forward 1 square	39. go forward 1 square
20. turn right	40. turn left

41. go forward 1 square

42. turn left

43. go forward 2 squares

44. turn right

45. go forward 1 square

Part 3

And now that you can combine your turns with moving forward, you end up with only 23 commands.

1. go forward 3 squares

2. turn left and go forward 1 square

3. turn right and go forward 1 square

4. turn right and go forward 1 square

5. turn left and go forward 1 square

6. turn left and go forward 3 squares

7. turn left and go forward 1 square

8. turn right and go forward 1 square

9. turn left and go forward 2 squares

10. turn left and go forward 1 square

11. turn right and go forward 1 square

12. turn right and go forward 2 squares

13. turn right and go forward 1 square

14. turn left and go forward 1 square

15. turn left and go forward 1 square

16. turn right and go forward 3 squares

17. turn right and go forward 1 square

18. turn right and go forward 1 square

19. turn left and go forward 2 squares

20. turn right and go forward 1 square

21. turn left and go forward 1 square

22. turn left and go forward 2 squares

23. turn right and go forward 1 square

DECIDING WHAT TO TAKE

→ if weather = rainy

→ then take umbrella

→ or else if

→ weather = sunny

→ then take bike

→ or else if

→ weather = snowing

→ then take coat